Library of Congress Cataloging in Publication Data

Hamilton-Merritt, Jane.
  My first days of school.

  Summary: Five-year-old Kate relates the
experiences of her first day in kindergarten.
  [1. Kindergarten—Fiction. 2. School
stories]   I. Title.
PZ7.H18284My   [E]   81-21361
ISBN 0-671-44417-4   AACR2

Designed by Meri Shardin.

Manufactured in the United States of America.
10 9 8 7 6 5 4 3 2 1
LITTLE SIMON and colophon are trademarks of Simon & Schuster.

Also available in Julian Messner Certified Edition.

. . . to Kate and her family, whose splendid cooperation made this book possible

. . . to all of Kate's classmates

. . . to Robert Bernstein, principal; Peg Vanderlip, teacher; Dolores Gerah, teacher's aide; and staff of the Redding Elementary School

. . . to the Candlewood Valley Bus Company and the Bee's Nest

. . . to Sturdevant's Photo, particularly Henry Deysenroth

. . . and to my most capable and good-natured assistant, Susan Snow.

Hi. I'm Kate. I'm five and Bear and I are going
to kindergarten.

Before school started, I had many things to do. Mommy and I visited kindergarten and I read the alphabet letters above the blackboard. I also drew pictures for the teacher.

Mommy and I went shopping for a new dress. I wrote my name on my lunchbox in case I lose it.

I get up early today because there's so much to
do before the bus comes. Mommy braids my hair.

My big brother, Jacques, helps me with my new
shoes. We fix my snack for school. We all eat a
good breakfast.

Then I hear the bus coming.

"'Bye Mommy. 'Bye Daddy. I love you."

I'm lucky because my older sister, Sarah, helps
me get on the bus.

I'm so glad Bear is with me. Do you suppose I'll make any friends?
My name and bus number are on my name tag. Mrs. Vanderlip, my teacher, says I must wear it every day so I won't get lost.

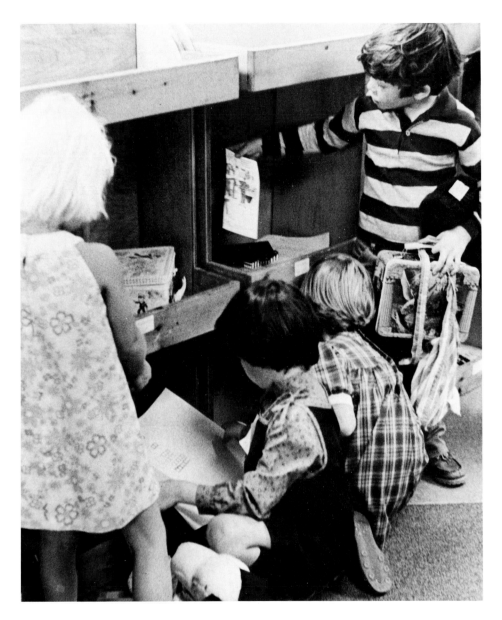

She shows us our cubbies and tells us that we must keep all our things in them. Then she shows us where the bathroom is. She tells us that we can go to the bathroom any time.

The teacher asks us to sit down. We take turns talking about our families and our pets. I tell everyone about Bear, my best friend.

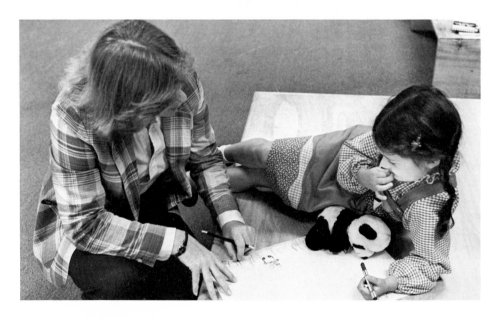

Mrs. Vanderlip gives each of us a box of crayons and asks us to draw pictures of our families.

While we are working, we have a surprise visit.
The principal comes to say hello.

There are so many things I need to remember:

to stay in line, to be careful on the playground,

to wash my hands before snack-time,

and to wait my turn to talk.

Today, we go to the school library. Bear and I
find a book about bears.
The librarian reads to us.

It's been a busy day. The teacher helps me get
ready to go home.

Bear and I have lots of things to tell Mommy
and Daddy tonight.

Everyone likes the picure I drew at school.
Mommy asks me if I made a friend. I tell her,
not yet. I tell about the boy who sometimes
cries. Tomorrow, I will try to be his friend.

It's the second day of school. Teacher says I have lots of work to do today and Bear must stay in my cubbie. I hope I make a friend today.

First we have art

and music,

gym,

and work periods.

I also have a special job. After snack-time each day, I sweep the floors.

After snack-time, it's play-time. The teacher
asks me to show the playground to the new girl,
An-Lon. I think she'll be my new friend.

I also ask Tyler to play on the slide with me. It's easier than I thought to make friends.